Snippets of Life: Prose in Poetry

Dr. Richa Jha

BookLeaf Publishing

India | USA | UK

Presentation by *BookLeaf Publishing*

Web: www.bookleafpub.com

E-mail: info@bookleafpub.com

ISBN: 9789363315891

First edition 2024

*To the two pieces of my heart, Shaurya and
Jaankee.*

ACKNOWLEDGEMENT

A big big thank you, to all who are going to read these poems. And a bigger thanks to those who have already read my poems and gave me the confidence to get them published. Avinash, Shaily, Shalini, Kshitij, Kaushik and of course, my parents and mother-in-law. All of them made it possible for me to write against all odds (mainly self-created, like laziness , procrastination, sedentary lifestyle etc)...a couple of these poems also owe their existence to a very dear friend of mine, who first proof read them, and also helped me with some editing. Thank you.

PREFACE

This book is not for poetry. In fact, it is for prose. To tell the stories that have been left untold, about women, about people, about ourselves, in this ever rotating, fast paced gyre, called life. This anthology is to tell the story of survival, sacrifice and victory. To talk about fate, fact and fatalities; Myth of Orestes, epic Mahabharat, emotions of a new wife, and old woman and a child. All find their little corners, in this small book of mine.

Draupadi's Agony

Is there an end to it, my Lord?
When will the rains of torment subside?
Probed fire filled eyes, her tears dried
Could agony in death equal agony in life?
Did all her penance still not suffice?
When, Lord, when? Heart smouldered in pain
Fervent glances kept waiting in vain

Father, brother, uncles and cousins hundred
All gone forever, at altar red
Sons too followed that path she dread
While the grandsire lay calm on his arrow bed
She looked on, tears welling and searing
Heart sinking yet pounding, resolve unyielding

Bloodbath sworn for revenge had changed
The world that she knew, perpetually deranged
Head from her heart been long estranged
Her Krishn alone knew how her soul was
manged

Death echoed, deathly silence jarred
The little pump still beating but deeply scarred
Beam of hope confirmed by midwife
At last, some meaning, in all this strife.

Little Grain of Sand

Grain of sand that stopped the flood
Lies on the shore trampled by all
It sought no trumpet, no songs, no ode
Its duty fulfilled was in itself reward
Can you be the sand and seek no glory?
Asks the man who glorified virtue
Seeking no reward per se
Yet getting all that was to gain

The woman smiled, her glory veiled
She looked at the man who stood by her side
Both exchanged that glance again
That said they knew the world behind
And thought it best to keep aside
Dissenting views, those winds that ruffled
Feathers best kept combed and bright

Let's see how long can the glitter be maintained
Of false ideals and thoughts waylaid
This world is good for those who know it
And better still for those who made it
Becoming a grain is not at all small
You stop the flood and fill them all
The problem is not of that grain in itself
As much as in those looking for a song

Where song falls short of expressing the greatness
Of a deed done for Dharma, in its purity, in earnest.

The Clarion Call

Green leaves and blue water
All fruits and meadows
Tall rocks and striking thunder
Far stretched land and seas and shores
-- We've got 'em, we should cherish,
For He loves the man,
Our greed will make us perish
We'll bleed by our own hands:
If we dig farther than His plan,
Powers greater than man shall rise,
Balance shall be brought again;
Earth will live with our demise.

The Orestes Myth

A thousand wishes stared at me
Accusing me, loathing me
What had I done?
How could you...did your heart not cry?
Asked the daughter 'fore pulling the dagger
And the son looked on....

Was this the deal I bet on?
Was it the life I chose?
Or was it the end all was for?
For this was all life gone?

Too many questions, all jumbled in flood
Of accusing glances, blood 'gainst blood
No, not yet ...not all was done
The worst was yet to be...
When all had gone, he wandered still
Chased by films
Not sure what's dead
And not sure what still lives.

He did nothing but think!
Who would have thought it'd come to this.

All his life haunted by the ghosts of dead
A fleeting thought daunted his vision, red
That one deed, which was in mind enacted,
His fate for eternity, for ever dictated

Aeschylus gave his play this twist
To placate the Furies that reside within
So men might know and spite resist
To think evil is equal to committing the sin.

The Poor Kid

His moist eyes gave away
Desert infesting his heart
Dry lips couldn't move to say
His words, muffled by the scars.

'Run away!' his mum had urged
He had stolen when hunger surged
Feeble legs couldn't carry him far
Caught he was - made bonded labour
Bought and sold like cattle with bell
Poor kid he was - too weak to yell

Hurricane of pain twisted and tangled all the
tissues inside
Warm water ran down both vessels when the tide
rose too high
-- And the man choking on his bread and wine
Immune to the heat of desert asked:
'Poor kid...is he mute?'
...the poor kid. He's just in pain, acute.

The Times of Corona

Days kept trickling down the saline ridges
Thumping of the heart now less, now more
Thinking of the journey that could have been
Of people unmet and sights unseen
Without the distance marring the joy of life
Living days unending in constant strife
In life without love and love sans life
Every breath taken, on the edge of knife...

Caregivers, oxygen, scalpel and scales
The world's either silent or screeching with wails
The times are tough
Have we really lived enough?
And the heart races back to open the stories
boxed in
Some were lived and some imagined
Of a together, that was never really joined
Always in tertiary that union remained
Now the salt in eyes rubs bitter
Thinking again of what could have been
Sweat that chills runs down the bridge and vales
Thinking forever of what could have been.

The Exiled Princess

The snake in her eyes rose to display
The fangs of desire she thought had been slain
She wanted it all -- the heaven, not hay
This time she'd try harder again.

For long had the martyr in her taken lead
High time that she paid her heart some heed
To battle the chains that held her captive
Inspiration had dawned in her word with the
native

If that frail little girl could show such courage
To fight all odds and break free of bondage
Surely she, who had once tasted limitless sky
Had it in her to live without being shy
Of her own desires and dreams and passions
Roses she'd given, now was time for some guns

She must reach out for her dreams, a little high
She did deserve more than these tears and sighs
No! The fire in her belly, she'd not let douse
This time she'd win all back - her real house.

Joys of Motherhood
Unbound

Her heart knew no greater delight
Than smiles that radiated into her soul
Of those little lips and shining eyes
Those tiny palms that made her whole.

Joys of motherhood she'd read about
Had felt it overrated,
Till fate decreed she had her own
Knew now, love couldn't be gated
There were no bounds, no limits to love
Her baby, she loved, way over and above
Every other thing in this world.

When silver streams ran 'cross her plain
And tears streamed out of contentment
She knew, she'd found her goal for life
There couldn't be any more resentment.
Ambition of a woman, a wife, and daughter
Of friend, and lover, a teacher and sister
All were pushed behind
The primary love, that primeval force
That ties a mother to child.

No, not sacrifice, this was her choice
To have someone who'd mean the world
Precious than heaven and earth around
Her own flesh and blood, out, walking the
ground
Sleeping and smiling, in her lap, curled.

Mothers down ages, seemed to be smiling upon
her
Pure joy and peace still made her wonder
Running her fingers up and down silver ridges
Those scars of battle, of life won in stitches
She smiled a happy smile as she saw what these
had got her
Her pretty little baby to call her own forever.

Misinterpretation of Dreams

Tolling from the hills beyond
the shrill cry of death announced
Shattered dreams, a
half-stitched sock, an empty belly rolled.

God's men had come and picked it up
To make it suffer more
Forced to live it dawned on him
Her wish still he could see through.

Chiaroscuro his life had become
For her, he stole and cried for soul
Evil and good lived in one.
The saviours fell short of pity
When he renounced all taught by them
Kept filling his coffers to prove
He could survive at helm

Mother never wanted this sin
His crimes a blot on her upbringing
She tried to stop the storm before flood
But it had to end in guns and blood.

Rose and move he did
This world, till the chimes echoed no more
Liberated he was of burdened life
Free like a kite without its line
She was punished for the early exit
Forgotten in (his) exile.

Rusted Ears

Words unspoken, lie on face, truth denied
Her inward eye shut brutally with force so tight
No logic, no reason, no clear stream passes by
Through the hole pitch black, all dark, not a
beam of light
To talk some sense, to show the world
As it should be seen without vision blurred
By illusion, beliefs and waylaid passion
For fancy, fantasy and everything magical.

The cool blue stream went dry too soon
Every promise made, falsified too soon
Heart calcified, long, bouldered tunnels
Winding in shadows, those waterless channels
Witness to tears turned stone, over time
The ocean of sorrow left salty and dried
High tide wakes a sleeping river with all its
might
Keeps her tossing and turning all morrow and
night
Not a moment of rest from thoughts evil,
villainous
Angst, impatience, frustration and envy ominous
Tools of depression constant at work
What's deadlier than viruses is an ear that's rust.

The Prophecy of Redemption

Two bits of poetry and a pail worth of pain
Brought him back to the garden that lived in
disarray

Strutting through this same spot, had he spotted
her first
His parched soul and browned tongue had asked
relief from thirst

He'd asked for some respite from the path
beyond this garden
For this world looked like a mirage, from the
desert he had long walken

She'd taken him in, into the house,
Served him food and water
Drinks were brought and marriage announced
For he'd fulfilled the prediction
The union would not augur well, she knew well
forth his visit
Yet, smiling from the lips she dressed up for the
'happy wedding'

She'd loved him. She lived for him,
The woman in the marriage

He, the man, had felt so big
Master, in holy alliance
Forgotten was her life saving broth
Unremembered, what brought their nuptials
Registered only the boon of man
The rights, commands and orders

Blood, bruises and gaslighting,
And voice loud like thunder
Echoed in that paradise, till it was torn asunder
Gone were memories of humble traveller
Tramping the world in hunger
Prophecy of doom fulfilled for her
It was time for her, she knew his fear.

Gone. One night. Without a trace.
The garden was left barren.
He looked here. And then looked there. And
thought of vows and duties.
Alas, too late did this thought come, he was back
to dirt and squalor.
Wandered here and wandered there, looking for
some sign divine
Gone, however, was kindness from world, those
hands that lifted thine.

No more recess from scorching sun
No elixir for parched soul in offering
Eyes empty, wandering, watering, wavering,

Searched for mirage, ever evading
But there was no one to help him now
Dead, the beautiful nun...

Once had treasured her, burning within,
Aglow with fire, engulfed in flames,
Had rejoiced in ecstasy, wishing the sun to never
set
That golden ball should always shine, wishes
fulfilled
Did believe he was God's favourite,
For him, He did exist.

Standing in the deserted land
Flooded with memories
He waited for the final call
To end his reveries
He would surely send bounty his way
Like she was saved from worldly chains
With bondage of love, he too was tied,
Till love turned hate and mercy died
Surely he, who repents day and night,
Could count on some sympathy
If prophecy worked its way like this
He'd wait for prophecy to fulfill
If the Gods that were, still there be,
He, too, redeemed, would surely be.

The Flight of Love

Rustling of leaves, and racing nerves
Silence of night, heart screeching verse.

Quick paced steps took her closer to sea
United with love, at last she would be.

Waves rocked the boat, anchored at bay
Long was the path to find her world gay.

She'd left what she knew for waters unseen
Life of her dreams there she had foreseen.

A little overdressed? Maybe, perhaps.
But the flight of liberation needs make-up, some
art.

Changed person, altered perspective
Lent her strength to stop being captive

Of social norms and general expectation
Had to unlearn selective education.

Had moved mental mountains to break the
conditioning
Hands that had tethered her dreams, her being.

Strength of the mind, steeling of the heart
Running to her love, was she at last
Sensations abounding, sensibility accursed
Years of shackles shattering, cursed metal
burst...

Saw her standing, where boats were moored
A lifetime of happiness, in her assured.

The Mother's Dilemma

She got no money, children three
Pauper for world, but rich with glee
She smiled at them, full of love and care
They were her own, results of her prayer.

Born out of love, a union divine
Not forced upon her, a sign of resign
Like she was for her mother, an unwanted child
Simply a duty, where expectations piled.

This joy won't buy her clothes, however
Need notes for food and drinks and cover
No real house would this delight buy
Sans shelter lying beneath the sky
She thought to herself, it's no matter big
She could always get back to do her gig.

Money she'd brought, she could earn again
But how could she leave them for some material
gain
The bliss in her arms, contentment in breath
Staying without them would be equal to death.

The man who had sworn to provide her for life
Had left for the nether world; she, no longer
wife.

She decided she'd work but who'd take care
Of her precious jewels, who'd treat them fair
Alas, she couldn't leave them yet behind
For expenses to meet, she made up her mind

To go back to him who had fathered her
Whose abode she had left to be hated for ever
With the man who loved but fate snatched away
For those who lived, she'd memory betray

Go back she did, not to him, to the shop
Where earned her children's father till destiny
dropped
A decree so disastrous that changed her life
Yes, a mother she was, but still a wife.

Dancing to Life

Life is a song without music so often
Occasionally melodious, at times, broken
Raspy, grating, jarring noise all around
Mind and heart engaged in a duel surround
Every promise made, turned to dust with time
Every act turned into a worldly mime.

Jingle of bells calls for mourning and mirth
Last rites announced, or celebration of birth.
Same sound, different meanings
Same person, different leanings,
It's all about time and position in life
Some chains can be broken, few get stronger
with time.

One man's life might signal someone's death
Baby's first smile comes from woman's last
breath.
A part of the whole she may always be
But never just herself for this eternity
No going back, no living for the self
Child is the future, for it, the present.

She, a woman before, but now also mum
Could never gather courage to beat the drum

The closet stayed locked behind little teddy
bears
A world full of lies, lived in lost dares.

Music in the ballroom, she danced before her
eyes, Swaying to music that didn't make her
smile
Clasped in love, spanning the floor
Strapped in heels, eyes on the door
Yes, saw her alright, standing still
These notes didn't sweep her.
Pretending.
Hurt. Was she? It was her idea
To move in this room, with strangers near
Probing beauty that was hers, Hers only, for
keeping
Yet lay no claim for fear of breaking
The image of a woman happy in marriage
In motherhood, in family, though living in
bondage.

One full circle, the last dance demanded.
Eyes fixed, he transfixed
And she, stranded.

Break the trance, the serpent seethed.
Lips quivered. She breathed.
Danced the last dance.
The swan song sung, enough for the day.

Not ready to be 'us' they parted their way
Once again dissolved in dusk, love locked away.

The Glorified Victim

She's called the force, the centre of power
She moves the world and blooms the flower
She births the children of all sex and race
Yet from their lot, does indifference face.

This indifference gradually leads to hate
Plans against her, seal her fate.
From her, even, language turns away
Night becomes bad and good is the day.

With her, are many such millions doomed
One voice quietened, all others groomed
Hushed tones, folded legs,
Hunched backs and bowed heads
Become the standard of her lot
Her station in life, always second,
Existence even, is called a blot.

Sweat, blood and tears,
Mixed with hurt, hate and years
Of humiliation, of pain excruciating
Used, abused and namecalling,
Every day taunts and gaslighting
Leading to generations of second class dolls.

Polished, gagged and put on pedestal
Pages of glory and talk respectable
Pronounced martyrs, their sacrifice normal
Nothing less from them to be deemed
respectable
In a society where hypocrisy rules.

The Lotus-eyed and His Beloved

He who has the lotus eyes
One who makes hearts blissfully smile
Saw the beauty that she was
In the garden full of flowers.
Knew instantly that she was his,
And hoped to take her home.

Broke the bow that she had lift
Aglow with joy all faces lit
His head with courtesy, tilted low,
Sought permission to wed the princess.

Daughter of Earth, turned golden bride
Taken away with lots of pride
By the greatest king, of his own time,
To make her, the queen of his son.

Welcomed, loved, adorned with grace
Bejeweled, beloved, in her palace
Sisters for sisters, she had brought, all said,
All rosy, reflecting the crimson of her head.

She knew her fate, he was waiting for the same
Till time would be, and calling came
Revelling in each other's arms, family bliss
Content playing house, till coronation was
announced.

Old king, senile, saw him going, holding her
hand in hand
Death came faster than expected, hope not left a
strand.

Magic in mundane they had found
Travelling throughout the dense forests
News came late of father's passing
And pleas to get back to the kingdom dearest
Lest all fall apart.

He, the son, and God incarnate
Knew duties called him away
No tears, no cries could help prevail
Nor his resolve could sway.

Man, wife, brother continued on their path
For which they had been born
Found their friends, defeated the foes
In process, from each other torn.

The ten-headed one could not defeat the love
that thrived on trust

One word alleging the king , however, brought
out the strongest gust
Flown away like flowers dry, their happy union
was
He cried, she bore with heavy heart
What a loose tongue could cause.

The daughter of earth went back to her mother
Boys left behind, to follow their father
In building a nation strong
Though all knew that he could not stay
Without her, here, for long.
Examples set, with the life he led,
His work on earth was done.

The Blue One followed Gold into blue
His duty on earth fulfilled
The Lotus-eyed swam back to her
Who the joy in him instilled.

Story of a Girl

The Story:

A little girl once dreamt of a prince in a castle
One early morn set out in search of him
Through woods and hay, forests deep and gray
She looked and looked, till she thought she'd
found him.

I saw:

....a little woman with anklets, bangles and a line
of vermilion
Tried and tried to fill mammoth sized gallons
Of boosted egoes and self absorbed conceits
With love and compassion wrenched out of her
being
She now just watched the Big Man stealing
Her worth bit by bit, her zest pinch by pinch
Zeal and passion dried up with crushed ire
Ways of the world has burnt her desire
To live the life she had dreamt of once
So much pain piercing her through, no will to
live
Anymore, defeated, for all her life she'd tried to
give

Yet, was pronounced a zero.

The shell of her core shelled out of the socket
Sucked and suckled, with empty life pocket
I saw her staring in complete neutrality
No, not submission any more. Would indicate
some vitality.

No stretch of green from heaven to hearth
All shades of pale stare back in mirth
Pots and pans, yellow, black and grey
Grimy, greasy, broken - all made of clay
Moulded, shattered, never had their say
Used, drummed, manhandled - night and day..

The Story (contd.):

Life has its own way of turning upon you
Dreams turn into nightmares when reality bites
you
The 'holy union' had taken all
She had, voice and opinions - chained and
gagged
Living on the edge of sword, hanging by thread
True love, as she had thought, now seemed
notion far-fetched.

A Little Love Story

Princess of her world,
Free bird with strong wings
Her laughter made all eyes shine
Full of love, her presence divine
Made everything nice and bright.

She walked in bowers, flowers bloomed
Her smiles brought showers in the gloom
Of happiness, her advent heralded
Well endowed, in humility grounded
She was all that one aspired
To make one's life fulfilled.
But she had her heart already set
On a mystic she had only once met
Last year in the cross-country meet.

His thoughts were novel, ideas fresh
He talked of change that she too wished
Of harmony, unity in diversity he spoke
His words inspired all the folks
To work for a better society

They both had known their love at first sight
Parents approved to their heart's delight
Only asked them to wait a year to be sure

To see it was not just imaginary flight
Of passions that in youth ignite,
This pull, they felt so strong.

A year went down, he did not come back
She did not doubt his love, it couldn't turn slack
Believed in him, knew well within
That something must be up
To be keeping him busy, away from her
So she set out in search of him..

Bade her goodbyes to parents grim
She had to go out and look for him.
Far east she went into the country
To find the man that she would marry.

She got to know how he had been
In the year gone by, what they had seen
Of the man she had chosen to wed.
The man had stood against state tyranny
Didn't flinch once when made a mockery
Now lived in exile, pushed away from the land
By the powers he'd sought to protect
single-handedly.

She'd waited enough for him whole year
His memories in heart, holding them dear
She had made up her mind to go and find

The love of her life on her own.
She found him working in a tavern
Through chinks that had some crack.
Serving and speaking, and still motivating
All those who'd listen to his track.

He needed love, he needed care
A co-dreamer wanted, as his partner
She quite ready to be all that and more
Went down on a knee with a question throw
Proposed. Explained. Accepted. Elated.
The young ones came back home.

Her love for him, the Warrior King
Was whispered in the ring
Surprised but sure of the daughter's choice
Her parents gave them their blessing
She lived happily, as free as ever
For the whole wedded life that followed after
Never once any regret chancing upon her
Dancing in ecstasy, flying higher and higher.

Love in Memoriam

She missed all of him....them...
The times long gone to never return
Silent waves crashing on the silver beach
Music streaming through the sand, she peach,
Entangled in each other, getting closer
With each swish of wind, falling deeper
In love, clasped in passion, never to break apart.
...with winged fancy, their proximity advanced.

She thought this moment would never end
Gods had planned a different story,
The road ahead had a steep bend.
Washed away with night, the moon's glory.

Careless whispers in stormy nights
Words never reached their station in time
Flown, waylaid from their destination
Deafened ears, anger, leading to frustration
Those words lie on those beach still
Echoing in the moored ships,
Looking for listeners, lovers again
Who'd take them to their journey's end.

She sits by her window hands on the sill

Head on the elbows, eyes filled
Wondering what went so wrong
Why words still floated all around
Why didn't they reach their port of call
How could their love have such a great fall
A thousand messages had gone
unanswered
With no hope left, her soul shivered
She wished for death, if life couldn't be
His sign nowhere, like sand washed by sea.

Nostalgia

Bigger homes and smaller hearts
Bane of this generation
Men will come and men will go
Building all the nations
But who shall take the onus of
creating relations sweet
Short of time and short of space, spewing words
of heat
The whole world looks busy
Darren, Gyaan and Suzie
All cooped in their holes all day
No smiles to give, not a moment spare, to while
away.

Getting farther and farther away from each other
Every day busy, the next day busier
No time to sit and talk awhile
No stories to engage and make all smile
Those days we had community gathering
Power cuts signalled rounds of chattering
People strewn like grass over the ground
Peanuts, samosas, jalebis found
In every group huddled, seated together
Those days were happy, bringing people closer.

No stress of modern media mess
Rare talks of depression, family dispersed stress
No telephones personal to break connection
One man's problem was everyone's tension
A world of community living thrived
Small joys, small talks, friendships revived
A simple smile could win the world
Unhidden under masks, lips curled.

A Song for the Kids

"Butterfly! O Butterfly! Where do you go?"

"I go over the hills away from the snow
Cold white weather tends to dampen my spirits
Warm winds and flowers I do need to visit
Colours and freshness lift me up in the sky
Give my wings vigour and power to fly
Out there in valleys and plateau and plain
I'll go make my home till summer comes here
again."

The little butterfly came to forest green
Stayed here with flowers and plants and trees
Made friends with insects, wasps and bees
Fed on the nectar that gave her more colours
Buzzed around happily till lasted the summers.

www.ingramcontent.com/pod-product-compliance
Lightning Source LLC
Chambersburg PA
CBHW061726130726
47996CB00006B/2529